The Dan Quayle Diktionary

by
James Wynbrandt

BERKLEY BOOKS, NEW YORK

Cover photographs courtesy of R. Maiman, Sygma.

THE DAN QUAYLE DIKTIONARY

A Berkley Book / published by arrangement with
the author

PRINTING HISTORY
Berkley trade paperback edition / September 1992

All rights reserved.
Copyright © 1992 by James Wynbrandt.
This book may not be reproduced
in whole or in part, by mimeograph or
any other means, without permission.
For information address:
The Berkley Publishing Group,
200 Madison Avenue,
New York, New York 10016.

ISBN: 0-425-13696-5

A BERKLEY BOOK ® ™ 757,375
Berkley Books are published by The Berkley Publishing Group,
200 Madison Avenue, New York, New York 10016.
The name "BERKLEY" and the "B" logo
are trademarks belonging to Berkley Publishing Corporation.

PRINTED IN THE UNITED STATES OF AMERICA

10 9 8 7 6 5 4 3 2 1

Introduction

Murfy Browne is a fictitious creation. So is this introduction. So is this dictionary. Incredibly, J. Danforth Quayle is not.

—Murf

Forward

My Fellow Ammericans,

   I never payed much attention to speling in school, but that all changed when I got to Warshington. Suddenly I had to spel out isshues, polecies, and even the long names of comittees I was on so I could find out where they were meeting. It wasent easy.
   Then Maralin suggested keeping a list of words that gave me the most trouble. Over time, I develeped speling tricks to help me rememmber lots of them—word asociations, visualisation techniques and other nemonic devises. Now I've brought some of these words and tips together in this diktionary. I hope it saves you some of the time and aggravation I endoored!

Sincerly,

J. Danfourth Quayle

On Using a Diktionary

A diktionary is a lot like our goverment—bloated and ineficient. I usualley need to look up only one or too words, yet I must waid through thousands to find them. And how can you look something up if you can't spel it in the first place? Its not so bad if you know the first leter, but how offen does that really happen? The simpel fact is, most diktionaries contane far two many words. Insted, why not have thousands of small diktionaries, each with only a few words? Then, if you have to look something up, you could go rite to the proper diktionary, and only the word you need would be there. This is the kind of bold and inovative thinking I hope to bring to the programs of the Edjucation Presadent during our second turn.

Aa

This is the first leter of the alfabet. I hardly knew it exsisted until well after compleating school. That keeps me working overtime on my A words!

AIDES
We're taking a lot of heat on this isshue—unfarely. We in the WARSHINGTON comunity have been paticularly effected. I will go public as others have, and admit that I have AIDES. I know the Presadent does, too. So we are simpathetic to others who have them. Especially if they are as INCUMBETENT as our AIDES. The increase in their numbers shows the federel goverment is out of control, and we believe the way to solve this problem is to elliminate all funding for AIDES-related exspenditures. If rellected, this will be our plan of inaction.

AJENDA
The Presadent says this is about the most important thing an addministration can have. Its like a big list of things to due. He dident tell me *why* it was so important, but he seems pretty upset that he can't find his.

AMENMENT
This is a way to re-enroll God in school. The biggest problem with public edjucation today is that God has left the classroom. He dident drop out, either—He was thrown out! But He has not been expelled, He is only suspended. We are going to bring Him back, so students can once again prey in school, and He can get His degree and gradjuate. Until then, you can't say anything that ends with AMEN in the classroom. That would make it a prear. We plan to altar the Constitusion so you can say AMEN and prey in school again. This is an AMENMENT.

I have devoted sometime to lerning to spel it. You may need only an hour or less if you use this handy tip:

#1 Think of God as a drill sargent, and He's just called the troops together, but instead of saying, "AT EAZE, MEN," he says, "AMEN, MEN."

#2 Then, for the happy ending to this word: You dident have to obey the drill sargent. You were in the National Gard, and while they were playing soldjer you were playing golff. You've just set your ball on a T.

AMENMEN + T = AMENMENT

Bb

So many eazy-to-spel B-words are getting wiped out of the diktionary, it's really depresing! B-1, B-2, even B-Happy...I heard the B-52s got back together, but I find that hard to beleive now that the Strategic Air Comand has dissbanded.

BILL CLINTOON
Again and again, I hear peeple talk about the caracter isshue of this man. I think I know what their wondering. What is his caracter all about, and how would it effect his performance in the Whitehouse? Is it a Batman caracter? Conan? A mutant turdle? Is he any kind of action hero, or just a guy from one of those romance comic books? I hope he's not planning to try musseling in on the Zippy the Pinhead persoana.

    I don't know if CANIDATE CLINTOON's caracter qualifies him for the presadencee. But I know it will have to be better defined

before he can succead as a comic book or annimated TV show I would want to watch.

BORTION
Real Reapublicans due not beleive a woman has the rite to have a BORTION. Especially if their pregnent. We get a lot of mail about this, so when I anser, my speling's gotta be ded-on.

DANS' HANDIE HINT

Rememmber that women shoud not have the *B*irth *OR T*ermination opt*ION*.

BUCANNON
George payed close attention to this wepon sistem during its trial stages, but once it dident work very well he kind of lost interest in it. This is a large bore, offensive assalt wepon designed to protect the rite side of our nation. It looked promising early in the development program, but proved inaffective at knocking out its target during field tests.

BUGET

Balencing this is nothing compared to the difficulty in speling it! "G" or "J"?—that's always the hard part. Try this tip and you'll never spel BUGET with a J again.

DANS' SPEL TIP

Think of how the BUGET puts the squeeze on taxpayers. Vwahlah—OJ rimes with no J!

BUROCRACY

This is the basis of our Ammerican way of life: A goverment of, by, and for the goverment. Self-goverment is one of the founding principals of our country. I have long suported the consept of a self-serving goverment. I think it is much more economical than one that goes to a table and waits for someone to come and take its order.

DANS' SPEL CHEK

The first cyllable is the hard part—
BUER, *BUR*, or *BEUR*? Its simple
when you rememmber the Ammerican
hero this is named for: Aron *BUR*.

15

Cc

C is a great Ammerican leter. Its the leter we lift our voises to in God Bless You, Ammerica, when we sing about a country where brotherhood stretches from "C to shining C." That's plenty far enough as far as this addministration is conserned.

CAMPAIN
This is what we endoor in our struggle for rellection. Grooling? Exausting? Humillyating? You bet, but so what, we're in it to win! I'm ready for the swet, ready for the challange. I can take it. Like they say, "No brain, no pain!"

CANIDATE
After the party nominates a person, they CANIDATE him or her. This is the prosess of preparing for ELLECTION or rellection, and involves assembling a team of handlers, damadge control experts, foto opportunists, and speling coaches.

COLLEDGE

To meet the challanges of a globel economy, we need a better-edjucated workforce. A COLLEDGE edjucation shoud be available to every Ammerican who gradjuates high school. That is, they shoud all have the opportunity to lern to spel this word. If you are asked during a job interview if you've been to COLLEDGE, your way ahead of applicants who say "No," if you can anser, "No, but I know how to spel it." Given the price of COLLEDGE, this is a cost-affective alternative. Use this hint and it won't take you four years to compleat, either.

We lern to spel COLLEDGE backwards. If you have trouble lerning things this way, get one of your frends in the federel government to help you.

#1 A COLLEDGE edjucation gives you an *EDGE*. But...

#2 First, your folks will have to put the house up as *COLL*ateral to pay for it.

COMUNISM—See RUSHA

CONSTITUSIONAL

To the best of my knowlege, this is a prosess or term that means a law is okay. I'm just a littel confused about it, because this is what my DADD used to say he was doing when he went to the bathroom in the morning. All I know is the Presadent wants me to go around saying the things we're doing are CONSTITUSIONAL. Well I know they are, because we've been shitting on peeple for almost four years!

COUNSEL ON COMPETIVENESS

Ammerican business has got to be able to compeat. Rite now we can't, because of neadless interfearance and reguleations from the goverment. The COUNSEL ON COMPETIVENESS is changing all that. Its really been exciting here at the Whitehouse since we put this team together. I'm in charge. George dosen't know what to make of it. I mean, one day I'm just a country pumpkin, the next day, hello, I'm going into outter space and shredding ENVIRE-MENTAL laws and making hoals in the ohzone. I mean, its like a total turnaround! I couden't due it without these guise. We're all on the same waivelength. They think the same way I would if I could think. They can argue around any law, find any lupehole, tie up any reguleation and drane any wetland. But that's not what I like best about these guise. I like hanging out with them. They're sharp! We go out for a few beers, and they start talking wild plans about how to toetally overhall the goverment, like, okay, the SOUPREAM COURT, who needs it, ha, ha, and then, all of a sudden, its like a rush cause we practicly could really due it!

Dd

I have been getting a workout on my D words lately. I gess its what they call our era of retrenchment. A time to D-escalate, D-reguleate, D-cafinate and D-fibrilate. Here at the Whitehouse, we have had to ajust our philosofee accordingly. For our second turn, I have suggested that we take all our polecies and put a D in front of them. In the interim, trueditional D words retain their importence, and continue to provide exciting challanges to spelers of all levels.

DADD

I'll never forget the day I became a man. The day I dropped the Y from DADDY. Looking back now, it seems harmless, but at the time, I thought I was being real rabellious. Of course, I talked it over with MARALIN first.

A DADD is a guy who can give you advise and permision, and pull strings for you. That's why I think they shoud be part of every too-parent FAMMLY. Too many kids will never need to spel this

word. But for those who due, our addministration is ready to provide leedership.

PROBLEM: Do you dropp a *Y* or an *IE* from the end to form DADD?

HINT: *Y* is at the *end* of DADDY and its also at the *end* of the alfabet (give or take four or five leters); *E* is *not* at the end of the alfabet, so it is *not* at the end of this word.

ANSER: Dropp a *Y*, not an *IE*, to spel DADD.

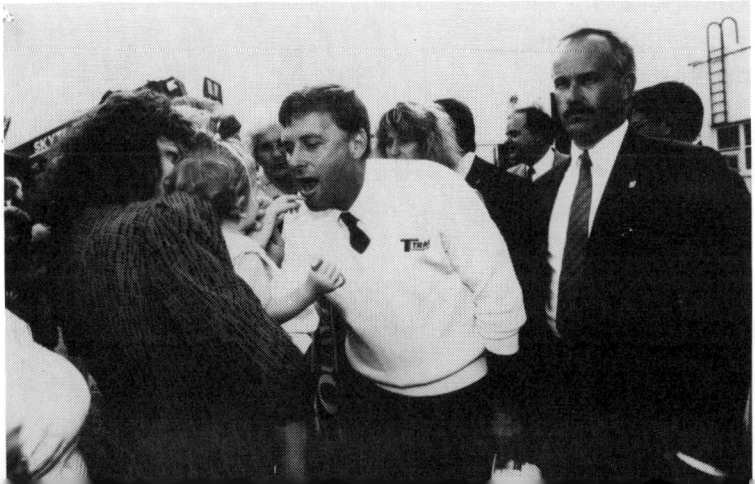

DEFACIT
This is not the way the finance comittee slouches and it dosent have anything to due with wrap music. This is what happens when we get through with the BUGET in WARSHINGTON. I found out a lot about this subject during my Frenchman year. I found out it may be dificult to elliminate, but it *can* be eazy to spel:

Think of a balenced BUGET as a work of art, carefully blending needs and resorces, as a Michael Anjello mite create a masterpeece on canvus. In Congres, this is what we due to that masterpeece. We *DEFACe IT*.

DEMOCRAP
This is the polecies, platforms and peeple of the loial oposition party.

DOMESTICK
Peeple say the Presedent is more interested in Forin Polecy than importent DOMESTICK isshues. Knot! What shoud be cleaned, on what days, how much carfare, and holiday bonuses are all the subject of frequent internel debate.

Ee

E words are very important. If we didn't have words that started with the leter E, think of all the blank pages there would be in the diktionary between D and F. Thankfuly, it would not be as many blank pages as there would be between R and T if there was no S. (If one leter had to be elliminated, I gess the least number of blank pages would be between W and Y, but who wants to live in a world without zylophones?)

E words are also important because some of the Presadents' major conserns are E words.

EL A
A new word! EL A is the largest city in the west, and celebrates its proud Spannish heritage in its name, which means "The A" in English. From a speling standpoint, its a pretty eazy city to live in. But the Presadent and I were sikened as we watched on TV while EL A was terorized and burned by a lawless, hate-filled mob. We will not rest until this Cultural ELEET is brought to justis.

ELEET

The Cultural ELEET is one of the greatest threats facing our BUROCRACY. We all know who they are—the Bush-bashers and the do-gooders, the tree-huggers and the bleeding harts, the haridressers and crossdressers, and the Hollywood set, from Murfy Browne to Mr. Ed. Need I spel it out anymore cleerly? The ELEET are:

- *E*nvirementalists,
- *L*iberals, and
- *E*ntertainment *E*stablishment *T*hugs

ELLECTION

I have been speling this one over and over, odd infinitem, working on it, geting it rite. I kinda beleive if you can spel a word, you can posess its sole, and that can give you great power. Please dont tell MARALIN I said this; she's a real strait arrow and anytime I say something like this she calls me "hippy-trippy," and rite now she's real sensitive about it on account of that guy whose in jale who's telling everybody I bought pot from him. She told me the first time he came over she dident like him, and she sure dosen't let me ferget about it now.

I shoud have it memmorized by ELLECTION time if I just keep this handie word asociation tip in mind, and invision myself in the voting booth pulling the lever for the *ELLEC*trocu*TION*.

ENVIREMENTAL

You can be assured that as dificult as they are to spel, isshues that effect globel eccologee are given lots of attention here at the Whitehouse. You can sum up our hands-on aproach in too words: ENVIREMENTAL Presadent. You can bet we're deeply comitted to the goals of perserving all things ENVIREMENTAL. We plan to continue to be leeders in this aria. But first we have to be sure we can spel it. Here's how I rememmber:

#1 Think of the leeders of the ENVIREMEN-TAL movement:
   *EN*emy

#2 Think of its impacked on our industries, our competiveness, and our stock dividends. Its like a:
   *VIRE*s

#3 Think of the type of person who worrys about a few degrees of globel warming or a littel hoal in the ohzone:
   MENTAL

Ff

Whenever I see this leter, its like I'm suddenly back in school!

FAMMLY
I've talked at length about the importence of a too-parent FAMMLY, and FAMMLY VALUSE. But to hell with that now. Me and the guise on the COUNSEL ON COMPETIVENESS were just kicking back with a few bruskees in the Rose Gardin, and here I am back up in my office, thinking, "I've got it all—the wife, kids, nice job," but, dam, if it werent for what MARALIN would say, I mite just toss it all in and give it a shot on the pro tour. Your laffing. You think I'm a bube? You think I can't due anything rite? You shoud see me on the lynx—I'm good! You don't think we're wasting taxpayer money flying around some weekend duffer, due you?

27

FREEDUM OF THE PRES

This is one of the most tresured of our Freedums, the rite of the PRESadent to due whatever he wants, and to heck with everyone else.

FROOTS and VEGTABLES

You don't have to write shopping lists to need to know how to spel a variaty of FROOTS and VEGTABLES. As a result of recent events, I have been spending more time working on the basics, the so-called meat and poetato words of FROOTS and VEGTABLES. That includes the "P" word:

POETATO

I got the message—
there's no E on the end of a spudd!

If your a beginner, don't try lerning too many F&Vs at once—the produce section is frought with danger for the neofite speler. Insted, try reffering to each jenerically as simply a FROOT or a VEGTABLE when you write. This may not be helpful when you're making out that shopping list, but it will keep you out of trouble. Like, let's say you're judging a speling bee, and there's a plant product you can't spel. After they spel it say, "Well, is that a FROOT or a VEGTABLE?" When they anser, say, "Okay, spel it."

Then you can judge them on that, and no one will know! Here are some common problems—and eazy solutions for F&Vs.

PROBLEM/SOLUTION: FROOTS

fr*OOT* or fr*UTE*?/
 I always put fr*OOT* in my mouth, like I always put my f*OOT* in my mouth.

*F*root or *PH*root?/
 You can order *F*root by *F*one.

PROBLEM/SOLUTION: VEGTABLES

TABLE or *TEBLE*?/
 The Veg is on the TABLE

VEJ or *VEG*?/
 Unlike froots, a VEG lays EGs

Ongoing financial burden/
 Presadents helth care pakage

FUNEREL

As soon as I got to be Vise-Presadent, I started geting innvitations to all kinds of fancy events all over the world. Mostly they were funerels. Natchrally, I had to write and thank them for innviting me, so that meant I had to be able to spel it. Thankfuly, only the first cyllable gave me trouble—the rest I knew by hart. But that first one…I kept getting confused, thinking my memmory aide was FEW, cause that made sense since there were FEWer peeple now that one less person was alive. But finally, I came up with the perfect trick: rememmbering that funerel starts with "FUN!" Because its fun to meet famous peeple you've heard about, even if they're already dead when you meet them.

31

Gg

GOLFFING

"What is it with Dan and this GOLFFING thing?" the Presadent asks my staff. They shrugg. They don't know. But where else does a guy like me get a chance to be humbel? I mean, I never had to work for anything in my life, knock on wood, but its diferent when I'm GOLFFING. The golff corse dosent know I'm the Vise-Presadent. The fairway and the green aren't impressed that I'm a world leeder. The sandtrap I get stuck in dosent care that the guy standing next to me with the briefcase handcuft to his rist has a secret code that will let me blow up half the world. The golff corse just dosent get it. Of course, the corporate presadents and poleticians I play with due, and they always lose to me on purpose. That oughtta send a message to the golff corse!

G

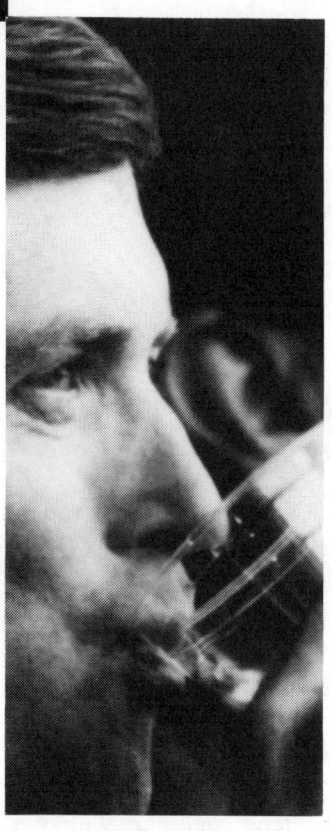

GROATH PAKAGE

I've rarely seen the Presadent so ajutated. He's waiting for delivery of a GROATH PAKAGE, and I think the shipping got all screwed up. Rite now its in Congres, and the Presadent is steemed cause they won't forword it to him. I dident understand what was so importent about the GROATH PAKAGE until the Presadent told me there were jobs inside, and that coud be vital to our rellection CAMPAIN… Oh…How due you put jobs inside of a pakage, anyway?

Hh

If you want to remember a word starts with H, just think of a football sailing over a pair of gole posts. If a word starts with G, just think of a golff ball being blown by a strong crosswind one leter to the left of the gole posts. It sounds crazy, but it works.

HANDYCAP
Having one of these isn't really very handy at all. I know because I have an eight handycap. I have struggled with it for some time, and with profesional help, I beleive I'm making ajustments to overcome it. Recently, the Presadent got a big new law passed that will outlaw discrimination against the handycapped. I'm glad. I hate it when club pros act like Godz or something.

HEARTBEET
This is how close I am to the Presadencee. Its closerthanthis. I can't help thinking about it. Presadent Quayle. When the Presadent got

sick in Japan, MARALIN and I talked about it. We wound up discussing how long to let Barbara stay in the Whitehouse afterwards, and we kinda got into a littel argument. I think a week is plenty of time, dont you?

PROBLEMS AND RELEEF FOR SPELING
HEARTBEET:

Can't remember if there's a silent *E* in the first cyllable?
Think of Presadent Bush hooked up to an
　*E*lectrocardeogram.

Which is it, a *D* or a *T* in the middle of the word?
Think of the prevalense of
　*T*hrombosis among men over 65.

Not sure if leters 3, 4 and 5 are *ERT* or *ART*?
Think of clogged
　*ART*eries from those high-colesterol
　Mane lobsters.

36

THE WHITE HOUSE

Dear Dan,

   Thank you for your note regarding my recent trip to Japan. I can assure you I feel fully capable of discharging the duties of this office and have no need to transfer authority to you, even for "maybe five or ten minutes" as you suggest. Regarding my physician's advice that I "rest for a spell," I can also assure you I am not preparing for a spelling bee, and therefore respectfully decline your thoughtful offer of coaching assistance.

Yours,

GHWB

H

HOMELISS

My name is Dan Quayle, and I live in a temporary goverment shelter. I've been here four years and I hope to stay another four. Its not so bad here, but its not really my home. Does this make me one of the HOMELISS everybuddies talking about? Maybe not ecsactly. Ask me again in January.

Ii

Be very cautious speling words that start with I and go back over the begining carefuly. Make sure you haven't substituted ME for the first leter by misstake.

INCUMBETENT
This is how peeple reffer to poleticians after they are ellected, but before rellection. They are INCUMBETENTs. This is an importent word to me, because this is how I realized I was a natchral-born poletician—peeple began calling me INCUMBETENT before I even ran for office!

INDYANNA
This is the state I was born in. That makes me an INDYANNA native, although I don't think I really look like a native. Not like the ones in *National Geographic*, anyway. Nobody in INDYANNA dresses like that. The state is named for a famed auto race and a vergin queen. I was born in the capitel of this state, a city that has more of everything INDYANNA is famous for. It is INDYANNA PLUS.

J j

JENIFER

This is some kind of rollaway bed or something for taking naps with. I think they're custom-made for peeple in ellective ofice who are always suposed to be werking, and don't want anyone knowing they have to take a nap now and then. Your not suposed to ask about them. Does the Presadent have one? No one here is talking. CANIDATE CLINTOON is said to have had at least one. I understand how that coud be a poletical libility. I must avoid naps, and only use my own bed. But that means I have to sleep with MARALIN all the time!

JFK

These are the inishuls of a statesman I am often confuzed with. In fact, peeple find us so simelar that when I debated with Sennetor Loiyd Benson back in '87, he had to remind peeple that I was actually *not* JFK—just in case they sudenly tooned in and got confuzed or something. The only way he could tell, he said, was because he had met JFK and worked with JFK, so he could state categorically that I was not JFK.

KWIK SPEL TIP

MARALIN says its eazy to rememmber how to spel JFK cause its the same as the airport in New York. But personaly, I don't see much resemblance between me and LaGuardia.

JUST SAY "NO, THANK YOU"
We have worked for four years to make this a kinder, jentler nation. Messege: We're polite. During our second turn, we are going to

J

make this a cornerstone of our federel drug polecy, cuppled with a strong interdiktion effort. If you are offered drugs and you due not want any, from now on just say, "No, thank you."

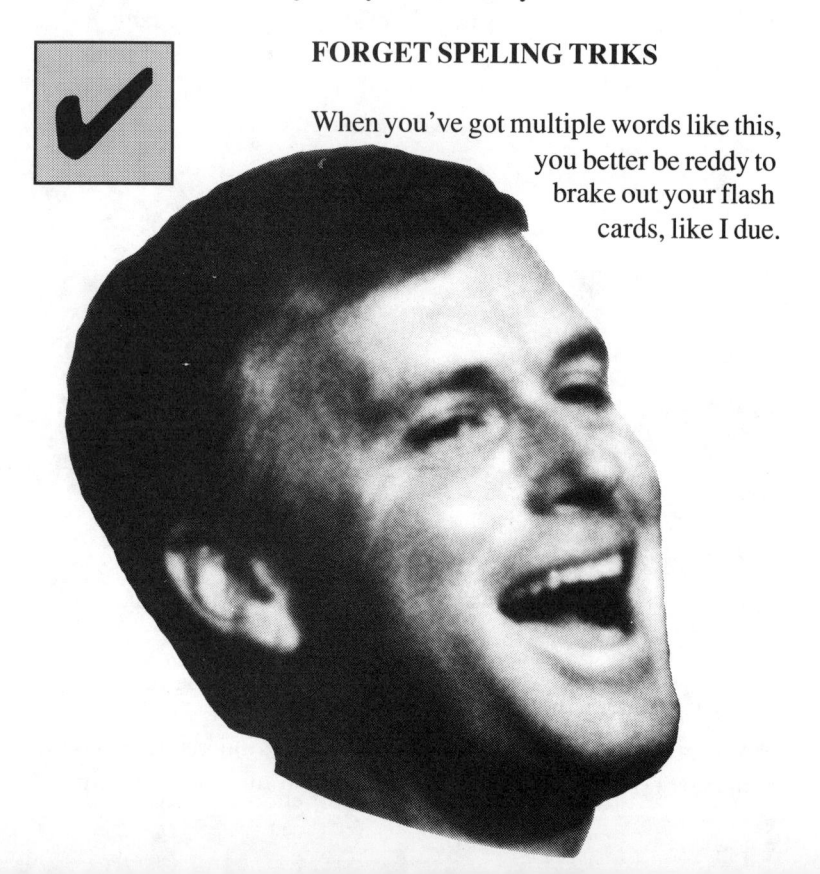

FORGET SPELING TRIKS

When you've got multiple words like this, you better be reddy to brake out your flash cards, like I due.

42

Kk

K is one of those unsung, plane-spoken, averege leters that make up the hartland of the alfabet. If the alfabet was Ammerica, I think companies would come to this leter to test market new products and convean focus groops.

KEN DOLL
I am looking forword to meeting this poletician some day. I'm sure we'll have much to talk about when our paths cross. My CAMPAIN manager says we are remarkabley simelar in both style and the way we think.

KENNEBUNKER
This is where the Presedent goes to escape the barrage of critisism he is subjected to in WARSHINGTON. The Presedent has a cigarette here. What else can you due while you're waiting out a barrage?

Ll

LIPZ
Read my LIPZ, the Presadent said. Was that a miscalculation? In hindsite, yes, but given how pourly Ammericans score on literasy and comprehension tests we just dident think very many peeple would be abel to read them.

The Presadents' handlers have made sure the problem of loose LIPZ will not be repeeted. They made a nice placard for the Presadent that can be removed pryor to his appearances, so his assistants can be sure he's ready to adress the public. The sign helps me rememmber how to spel this word, too. It mounts directly on the Presadents' chest with an arrow pointing up at his mouth, and says: Lie Indicator—Please Zip!

LOBBIEST
When I was a sennetor, I spent many hours meeting with high-priced LOBBIESTs, and interseeding for the special interest

groops they represented. Yet in all that time I was never called on by a single LOBB or a LOBBIER. I don't mean to brag, but I gess they only sent senior peeple to see me.

LOIALTY

This is the most important quality a Vise-Presadent can have. A Vise-Presadent has got to stand behind the Presadent, no matter what. A dog would make a good Vise-Presadent. They are extreamly loial. But a Vise-Presadent must also be abel to become Presadent, and that's something a dog wouldn't be so good at. Maybe if it was as smart as Rin Tin Tin, but I'm not so sure that was a real dog at all. I think maybe he was just an acter like our last Presadent.

Mm

If someone was to ask me why I like M, I gess the mane reasen is because you can't spel it backwards. And even if you spel it upside down by misstake, peeple will just think your speling a W. That makes it a very convenient leter to use if your not sure of the corect one.

MARALIN, MARALYN, MARYLIN, and MARILIN
Many well-known peeple have had this name, and all of them have been dificult to spel. I think of my favorite screen actress, MARALIN Monroe, or Judge Thomas's favorite, MARALIN Chambers, as well as other famous MARALINS, including MARALIN Fizzwater, the state of MARALIN, and of course the Second Ladie, MARALIN.

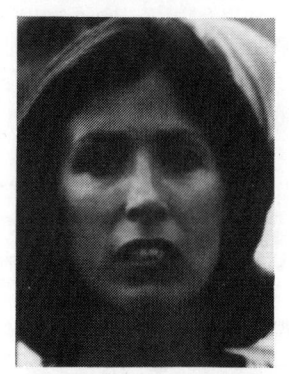

The problem from a speling standpoint is obveous: a jumbel of potential A's, I's and Y's clustered around the L in mid-MARALIN. To rememmber the three leters between MAR and the N, I simply say "MARALIN is *A L*adie, *I*ndeed" —*A-L-I*!

I'm working on something a littel more apropriate for Mr. Fizzwater. In the meantime, I also have episoads where I get confused with my nemonic and think that "MARALYN is A Ladie, Youbet!" or, more comonly, that "MARYLAN is Yelling Loudly, Again."

MARY O'QUOMO

I'm trying to find out more about this man—I may have to face him in the 1996 Presadenshell ELLECTION. He would be a nobel advarsery. Even though I think he's a pansy. So far I haven't found out very much. It will help my research imesurably if I can spel his name corectly. He has complaned more than once about the way I mispronounced it—he thought I was doing it on purpose! Oh well, at least I know how to get his gote.

M

✔

The speling problem: What comes after the O'? Is it a C, K, or Q? Ask yourself this series of questions, and the ansers will tell you:

Is "*O'K*womo" OK?
  —He's not OK in my book!
Then "*O'C*uomo" is rite.
  —Oh Contraire, he's way left.
Then it must be "*O'Q*uomo."
  —Un Questionably!

MIAs

What's the big deal? Am I missing something, or what? Who cares about some old military equipment that was Made In Ammerica? If its been sitting in Azia all this time, its probely rusty and obsolete anyway!

MILLY

Barbara and the Presadent have too Springer Spanniels. Milly is Barbara's dog. Vanilli belongs to the Presadent. Even though she's only a dog, Milly got real famous when she wrote a book recently. It was a best-seller! Unfortunetly, it turned out Milly dident really rite the book at all, and she had to give back her Grammie. I dident know what to say to Barbara about it, so I just pretended like nothing happened. So did she.

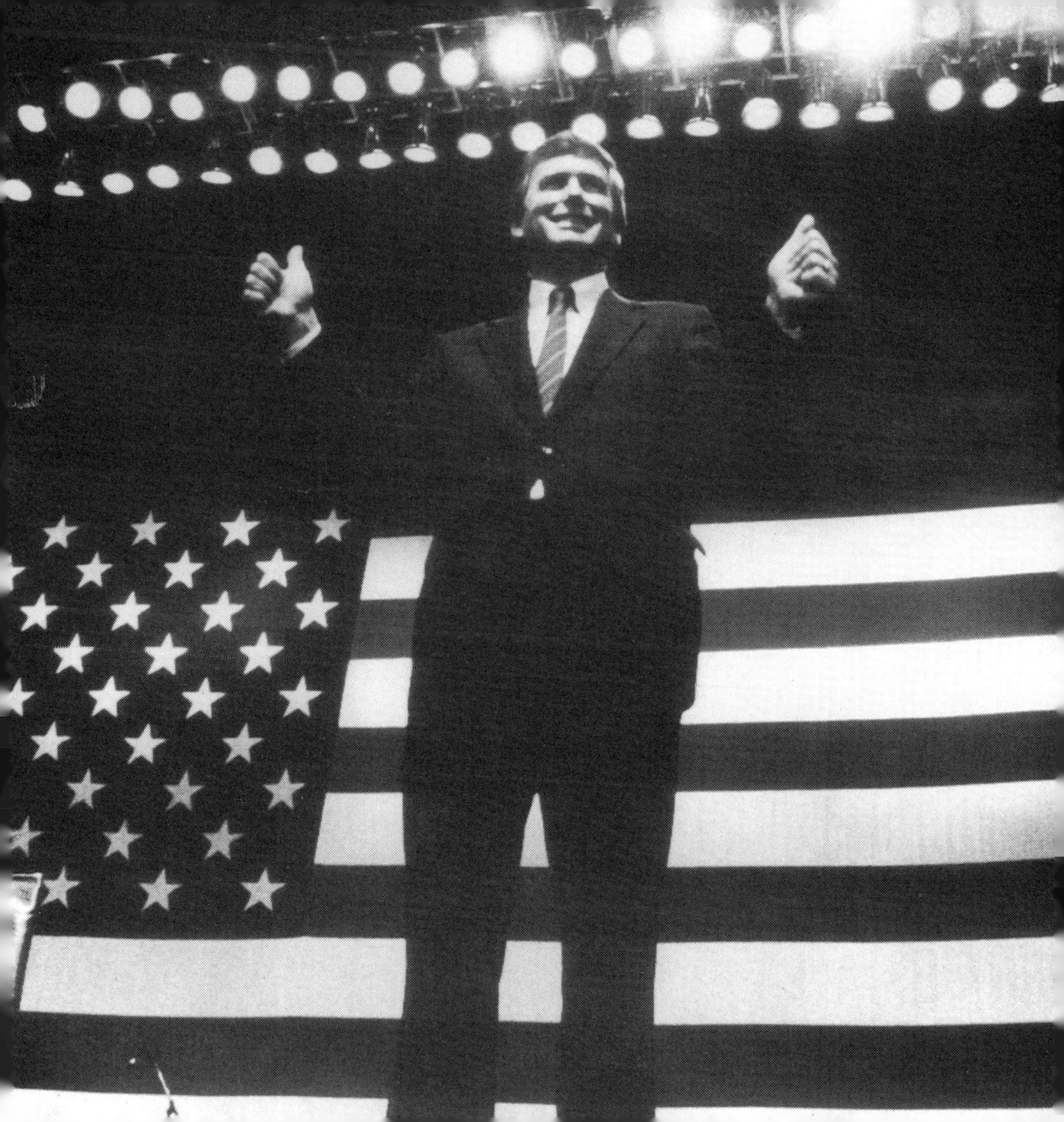

MYNORITY

MYNORITYs are all the groops simmering in the Ammerican stockpot. They are the various meats and VEGTABLES, the spices and seasonings, but not the broth. I expect by 1996, after another four years of our addministration, they will have been brought to a boyle. At that point, I hope the rite wing of the Reapublican party will be eager for me to serve them.

That is why it is important for me to adress the MYNORITY isshue now, and make it part of my 1992 CAMPAIN theme. Here's what I think: Could the goverment due more for MYNORITYs? In all fareness, yes. But my frends, this is not the responsibility of goverment alone. For they are not only MY NORITYs, they are YOUR NORITYs, too. They belong to all of us. Therefore, we shoud sell them to private industry, so that this resorce can be enjoyed for both commerical *and* recreational use for many years to come.

SPEL CHEK

If you have trouble speling words with vowels, try using words that have only consonents.

Nn

The leter N reminds me of myself. Because if M was the Presadent, N would be the Vise Presadent. Think about it—if M got wiped out of the alfabet, what leter would you pick to replace it? N has been there serving behind it all the time, watching, lerning. It could grow into the position, if the other leters gave it a chance.

NAVEL OBSERVITORY

This is my Official Residense, and I guess the name is suposed to be like an in joke, because the Vise-Presadent dosent get to due much more than sit around contumplating his or her NAVEL. Well, I've been contumplating at this house for almost four years, and I haven't seen many NAVELs, dispite its name. However, I herd my staff saying they've seen a big asshoal running around here. I'll just watch my NAVEL, thank you!

N

NEMONICS

These are triks to help you rememmber things—like the triks I use to help me spel! Peeple are surprized at my fasility for develiping unexspected analagees, word asociations and other NEMONIC devises. But you shoud see my boss! Here's a guy who was floating in the Pacific after his torpedo bommer was shot out of the sky, and when peeple ask what was going through his mind, he says he thought about the seperation of church and state.

NO VEMBER

After I was ellected to Congres I made a puzzeling observation about Presadenshell poletics: The ellection is always held in the same month, rite after October, yet there is not an ellection every year. *How could this be*, I wondered. I studied the calender and found the anser: There is a special ellection month added during leep years! On the other years, the calender simply says there is NO VEMBER. I dident have to look at the calender this year to know there's going to be a VEMBER. I have felt the excitement, and herd the Presedent say he is getting ready to go into his CAMPAIN moat.

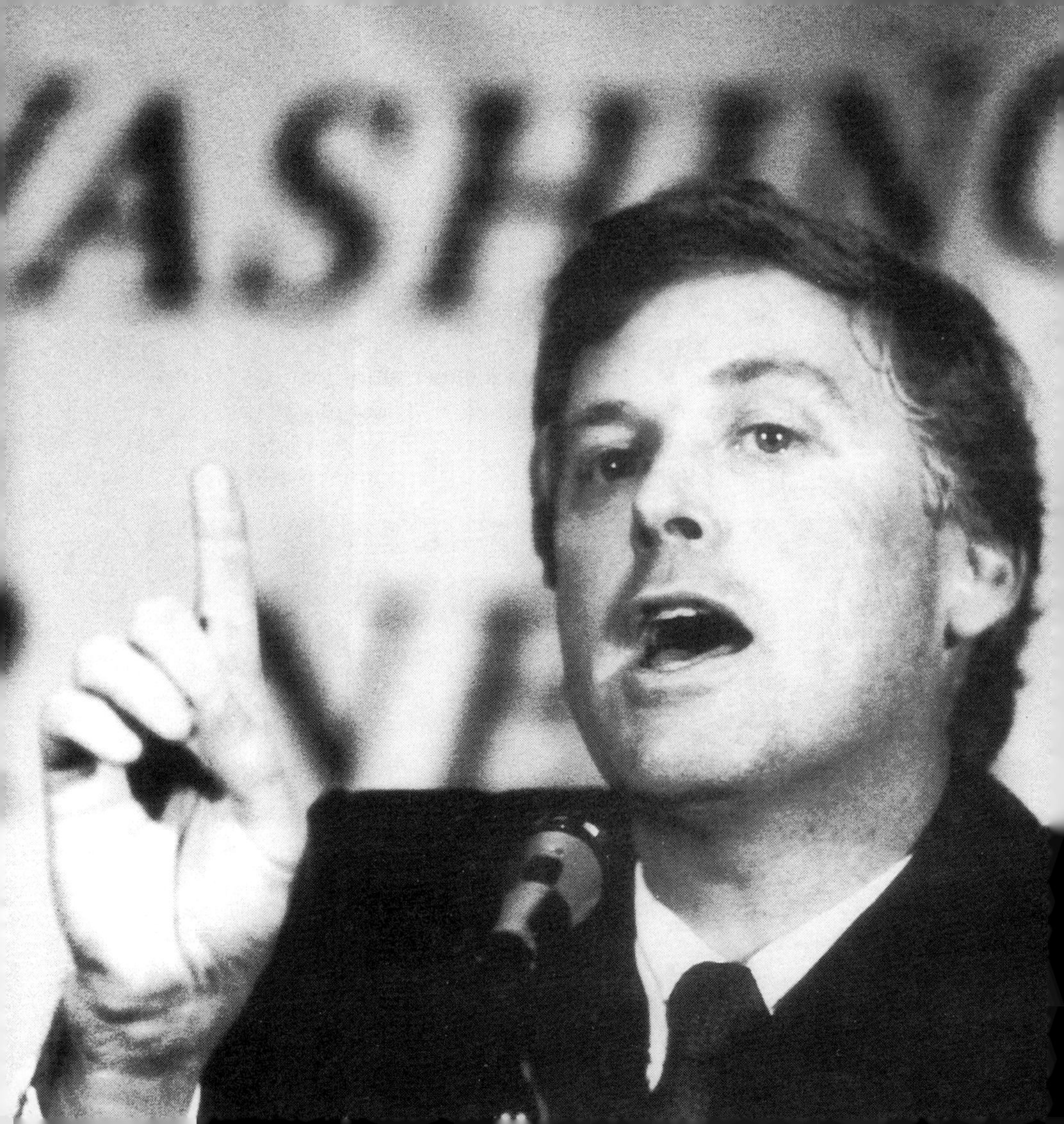

Oo

This leter is the first word in our National Anthum. I rememmber how strange it looked all by itself the first time I saw the words to the song. Now, every time I see "O" at the begining of a sentence, I wonder if there's going to be a space and then "say can you see" rite behind it. Once, I was reading this pome called the Star Spangeled Banner, *and it actually happened. It was like the* Twilight Zone *or something!*

OFFAL OFFICE
This is the Presidents office.
It reaks of power.

55

OUTTER SPACE

I have made OUTTER SPACE a major aria of my consern. It is a big place, but most of it is empty. The Presadent has encuraged my interest in this aria. Know what? He said I could be a crewmember on the first unmanned expedition to Mars! The Presadent has set an ambishus schedule for this project, and would like to see us liftoff before NO VEMBER. I've got to be able to spel this by then if I want to send postcards. I'll be ready!

SPACED OUT SPEL CHEK

One word or too? Imagine a countdown, and there's a malfunction, stopping the countdown on T minnus 2 seconds. That's it: Too words. You can start the countdown from wherever you like; T minnus one hour and counting is a good round number.

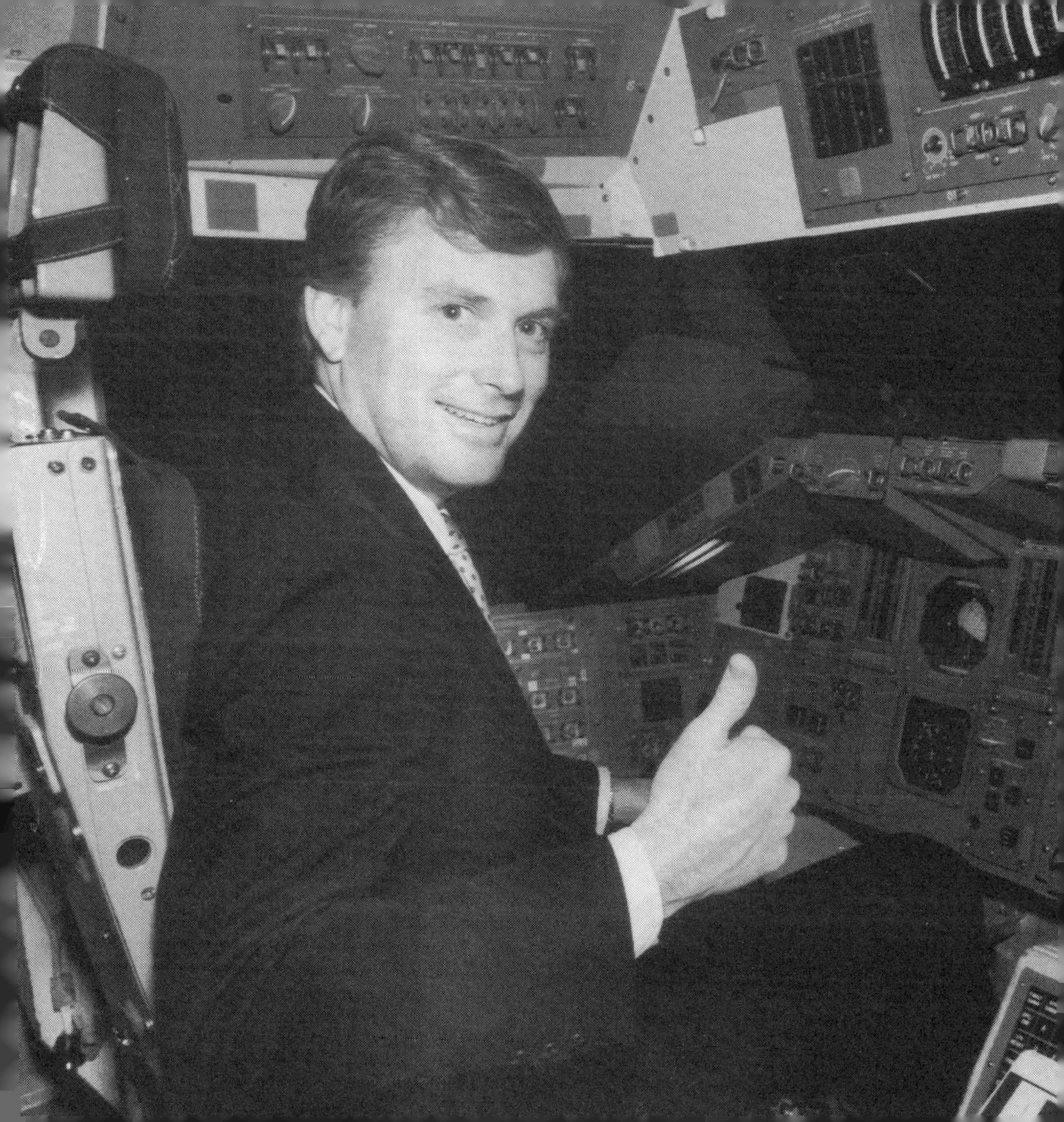

Pp

After George asked me to be on his ticket, I knew there'd be a whole lotta new words I'd have to spel. I put together a list of them, and here's one that really surprized me. You've probably seen our Comander In Cheif reffered to as the PREZ, and assumed that there's a "Z" in his title; but I can assure you, there's no "Z" in PRESADENT! I came up with this memmory aide to help me rememmber:

> *No siree, no siree,*
> *There's no Z in the Presadencee!*

(The trick is in rememmbering that it starts with "No" siree, not "Yes" siree; once you've got that down, its smooth saleing!)

PERROT
This proud and colorful bantamwait creature delights in being the center of attention. However, if you live with one, be prepared for constant squawking and periodic investigations into your background—the PERROT's feathers are easily ruffled. It feeds primarily on no-bid goverment contracts and it is found in TAXAS and WARSHINGTON, D.C.

POETATO
See FROOTS and VEGTABLES

POLETICS
My boss is the ultimate veterin of POLETICS. This is a range of nervus spasims and twiches you get from being repeetedly pummeled in public opinion surveys.

To spel POLETICS, just think of the onset:

#1 First you get clobbered by the *POLE*s,
#2 then come the *TICS*.

P

PURSIAN GOLFF

When I was first breefed on the threat posed by Sadim Hussain, I was shockked. I dident even know this variation of the game exsisted, and I thought I knew everything about golff! But I knew we had to perserve freedom in the golff aria, wherever it may be. The question was how, and I senced George was looking to me for ansers, as the addministration's golff expert. Fortunately, George plays horseshoes, so he dident have a clue either, and I was able to get through our first meeting using generel knowlege of the game. I assumed most of the rules were the same, but being as they played in the dessert, I figured they must have some monster sandtraps. I told George it was vital to avoid these, and reminded him that its best to bring your big irons when you're on an untried corse. I knew the game was over when I heard Sadim was trapped in a bunker for days.

So far, I have not seen the ferocious style of play asociated with PURSIAN GOLFF making inroads on Ammerican corses, but I beleive knowlege of how its speled is going to become de rigor.

PURSIAN GOLFF CRASH CORSE

#1 Picture a Purrsian cat. It *PUR*s.
#2 Imagine Sadim Hussain in Yule Brenner's role in *The King and I,* which was set in *SIAM*.
#3 Fantasize a new *N*d to this story, so that Sadim Hussain dosent live happily ever after.

[PUR] + [SIAM] + new Nd [N] = PURSIAN

Nothing too it!

Qq

Q is one of my favorite leters, and not just because my last name begins with it, either, honest! I like Q because you always know its going to have a U after it, so its like you've got a headstart on speling the word. But its more than that. How could you mind your Ps and Qs if there was no such leter? Without Q, our students would be able to study only half as hard, with disastaurous conseqwences for our globel competiveness.

QUAYLE

This is my fammlies' name. It is also the name of a kind of egg. It is also the name of a kind of bird that lays the egg that has this name. After my speech when I excepted the nomination for Vise-Presadent, I herd George say I lade an egg. I figurd it must be like fate—a good omen!

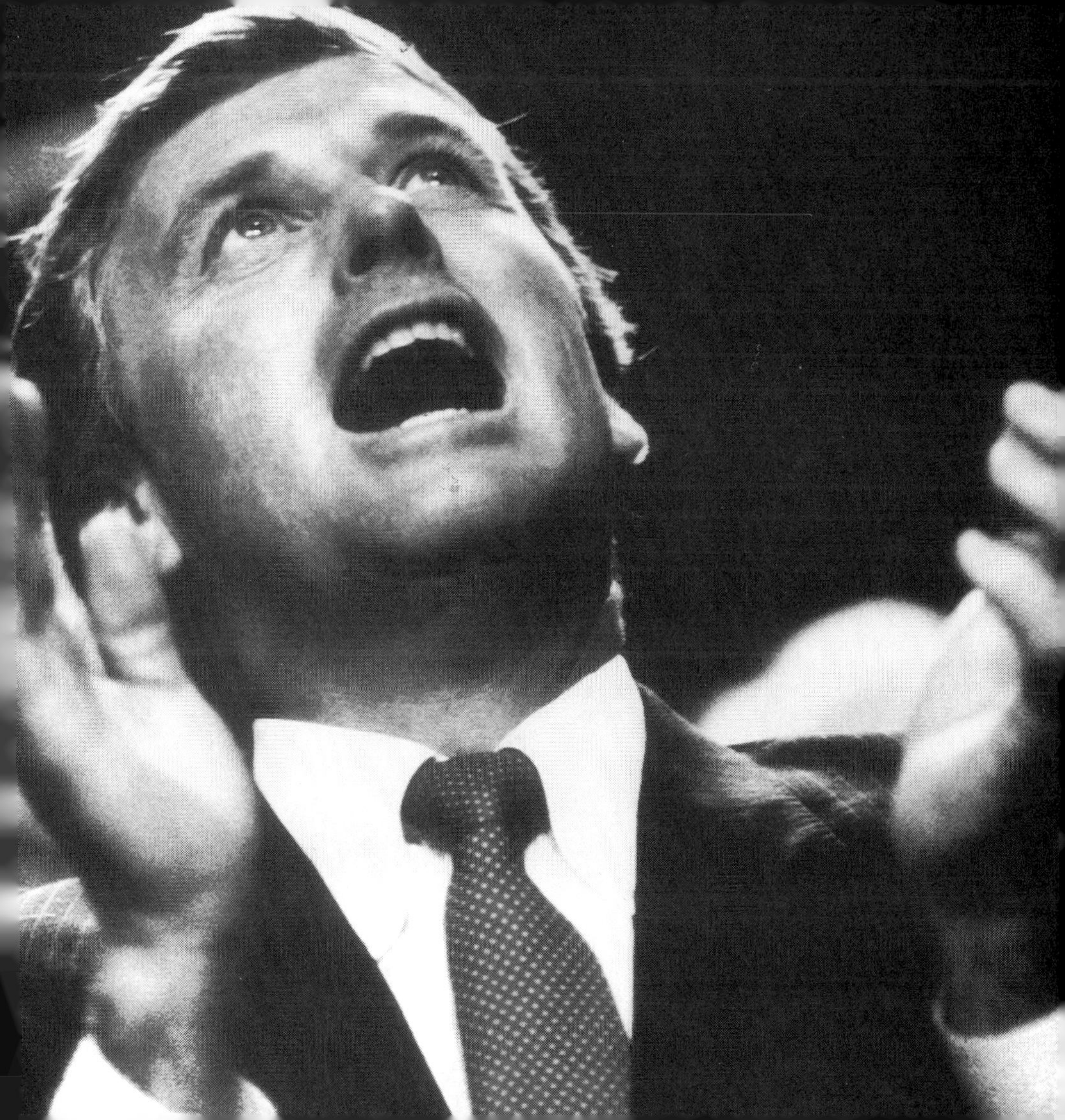

QUEAR

I used this one a lot with the guise at Delta Kappa Epsilon, but we never had to spel it. And we never imagined a day when some extremists in the gaye comunnity would wear it as a badge of honor. To a digree, I can empathise, because I like badges, too. ("Scorn" kinds are my favorites.) And while I've used this turm around the house for years, today I must be ready to use it pubicly, in a poletically corect manner.

I will not sherk this duty. Let none of these individuel's be misstaken: We welcome their use of this word, speled corectly, for the God-given intention it was intended to be used for: An ajective describing something that's not rite, be it an od coinsidence or a sexual exscapade.

KWIK SPEL TIP:

MARALIN came up with this one. She says, "Just visualise that it rimes with 'hear.'"

Rr

This is the most importent leter in edjucation, the leter of the three Rs: Reeding, riting and rithmatic. I think maybe they shoud make speling the forth R. Perhaps driver's Ed coud be the fifth. There shoud be ellective R's, too, so our students have a well-rounded edjucation.

RASICM

I have a dream. A dream of a big country club called Ammerica where everyone, no matter what race or religion, is free to ask for a membership application. I was raised in a world of such tolerance, so I consider myself in the vangard of this struggle. Some of the greatest sivil rites battles of our time were fought on the grounds of country clubs.

But now we must end the devide seperating those who belong to the club from their gests. We cannot allow a few disenchanted members who are behind on their dos to disrupt the facilities for

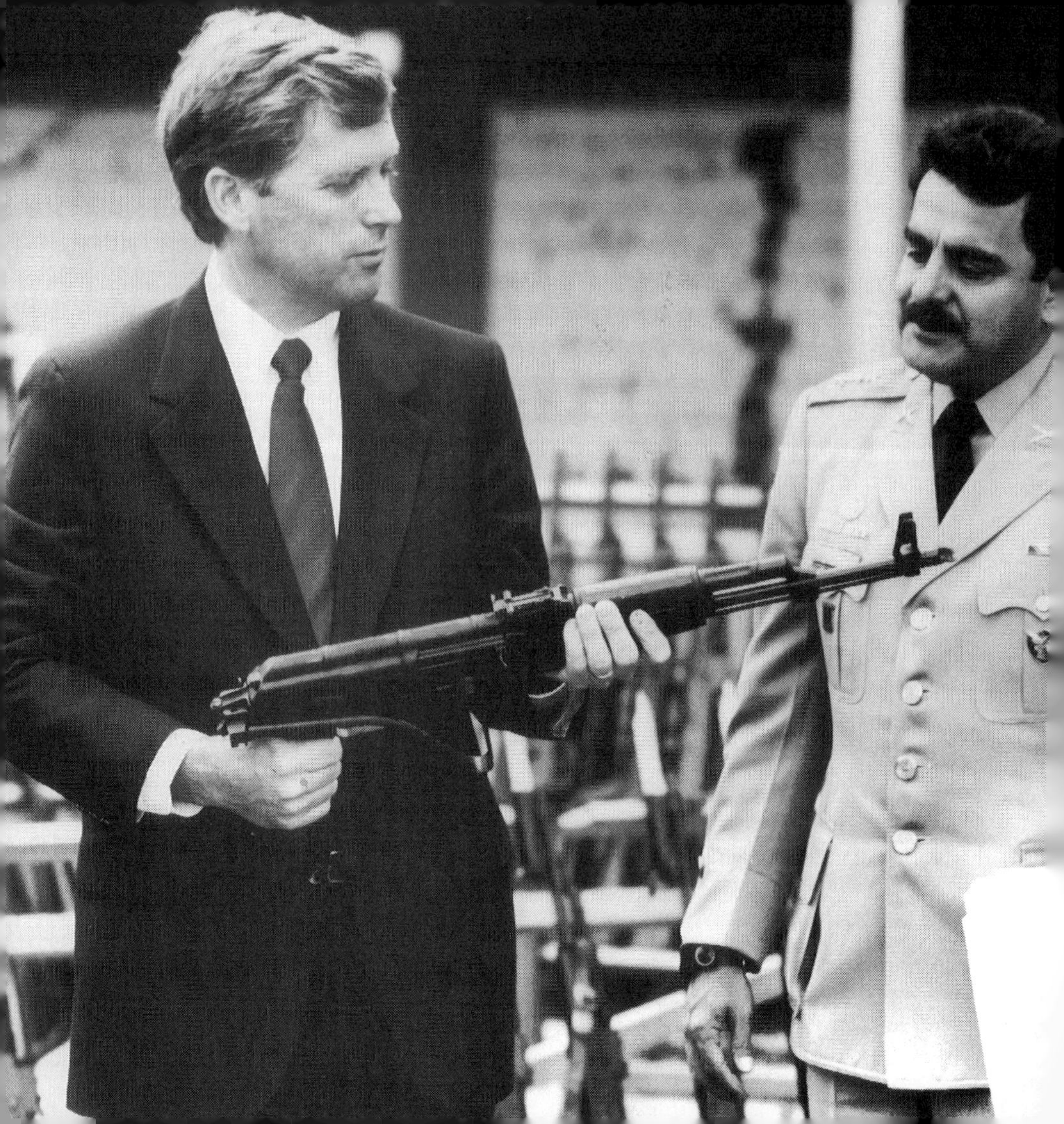

everyone, or presipitate a one-time assessment. My frends, now as never before, this country needs a heeler. And I can be that heel.

REGULEATIONS
I had many problems with REGULEATIONS until I came up with an eazy solution—elliminate them altogether. I'm getting help from the COUNSEL ON COMPETIVENESS in solving this speling problem.

RESESSION
This is something when the economy is bad. It is not hapening now. Rememmber the recent RESESSION? The one that's not hapening anymore? Its too bad it ended—otherwise no one would know we had a RESESSION. The Presedent told me its hard to evaluate the numbers when your in the middle of one of those things. Its only once you're out of it that you can tell. I feel like we're plenty out of it around here, so the Ammerican peeple can be confidant of our ability to know if we're having one of these things or not.

RUNING MATE
Beleive me, I was just as surprized as the rest of Ammerica when Vise-Presedent Bush asked me to be his RUNING MATE at the Reapublican Convention in '87. I wanted a little time to discuss it

with MARALIN, and after thinking about it carefully, I told him yes. The desision wasn't as automtatic as you might think. I mean, true, I played golff and was 20 years younger, but he was a real fisical fitness nut! Well, to make a long story short, we never did jog together. The next thing I knew, he announced to the convention that I was his nominee for Vise-Presadent. To this day, I wonder if he would have selected me if I had declined his offer to go runing.

RUSHA
Thank God the Evul Umpire has collapsed—whoever he was—I could never spel URSSRS worth a dam! I'll be forever indetted to Premeir Gorbachop for making my speling life eazier. And that goes for comunism in generel!

Ss

SAVINGS ALONE CRYSIS
In the early '80s, Presadent Reagen and Congres untied the hands of Ammerican business. But there was one problem: While companies from Wall Street to Main Street could stick their hands in peeple's pockets, some banks were still only allowed to make money on SAVINGS ALONE. It made it dificult for them to contribute to poletical CAMPAINS. Ledgislators on both sides of the isle worked very long and hard to end this CRYSIS. And now the public says we were asleep while all this was going on!

SOSIETY
This is the thing that is threatened by the Cultural ELEET; its the same thing that used to be threatened by comunism, and before that, by Atila the Hun, and before that, by the dynosores. Do not confuze this with the Great SOSIETY—our CAMPAIN intelligents operatives recently discovered that was not a SOSIETY at all, but a plot to destroy regular SOSIETY through a long-range program of pre-scheduled comunity events.

S

Getting a grip on SOSIETY:
Speling SOSIETY isn't much eazier than saving it. You know theres an E in there somewhere, but are there too Es or is there only one, and is it after the first O, or later on?

Solution:
Think of what the Cultural ELEET and the dynosores and Atila the Hun are doing to SOSIETY. S.O.S. immeadiately comes to mind.

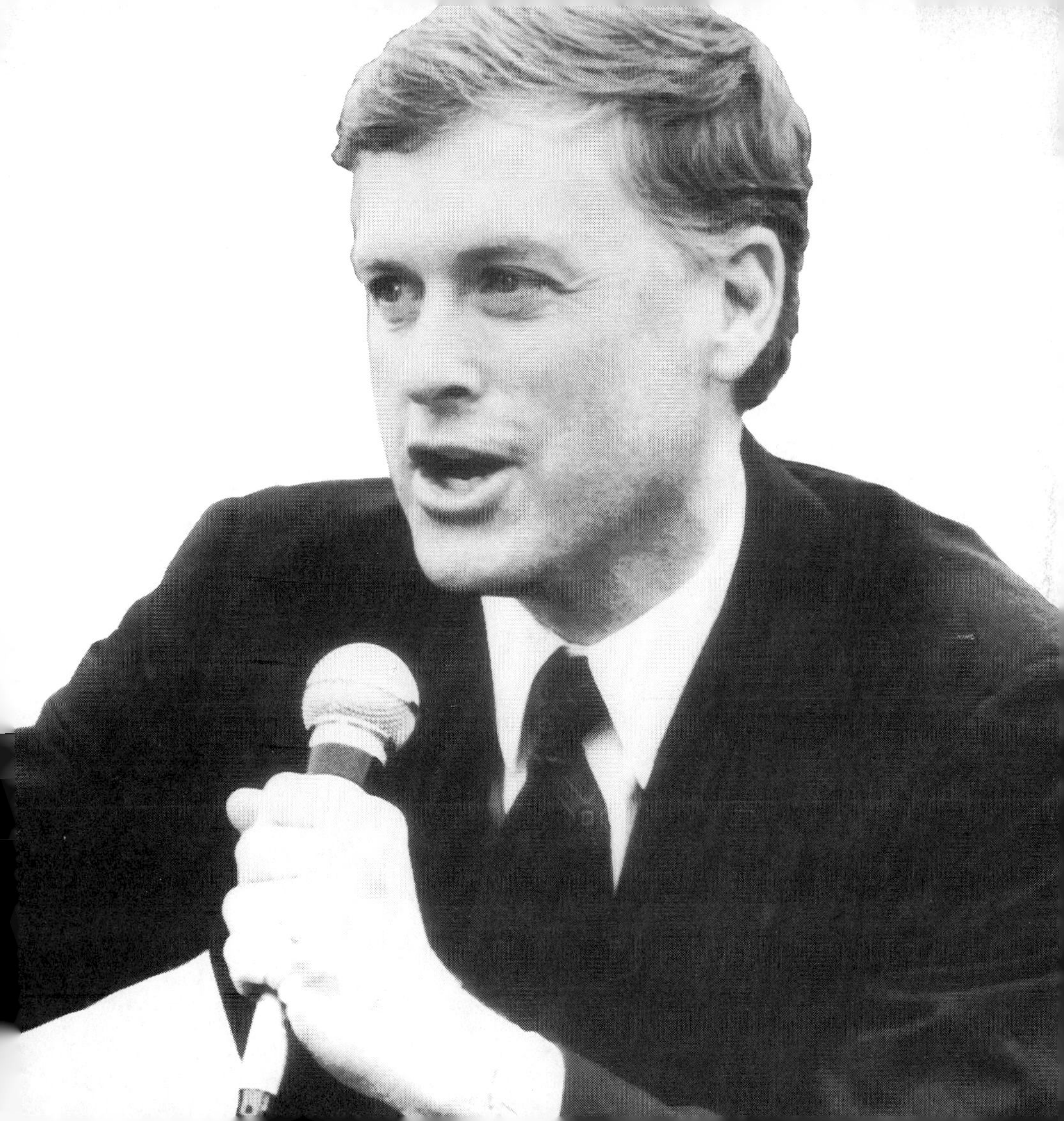

SOUND BITE
This is a small puncture wound made by a verbul gaff. Usualley they don't leeve a mark, and they go away in a day or too, but I've had 'em where like my whole body was covered!

SOUPREAM COURT
Let's be glad none of the Democraps thought to ask Judge Thomas to try to spel this one during his conformation hearings—its a tuffy! Most peeple immeadiately write "Soupreem" or "Supream," but I've got a sure-fire tip so you'll never mispel SOUPREAM COURT again: First, visualise the long flowing garments and the incredible powers of the justises: Think of SOUPerman. For the second part, think of what's going to happen to Ammericans who come before the SOUPREAM COURT when we get through with it.

SPIN CONTROL
This is the last sycle our dirty laundry goes through before it gets hung out in public.

SPOTTED OWEL
This is the reason why this addministration suports the logging of vergin forrest in the Pacific Northwest. Envirementalists in this area say they have SPOTTED OWEL. If these recloosive birds are so eazily seen, they cant be too indangered.

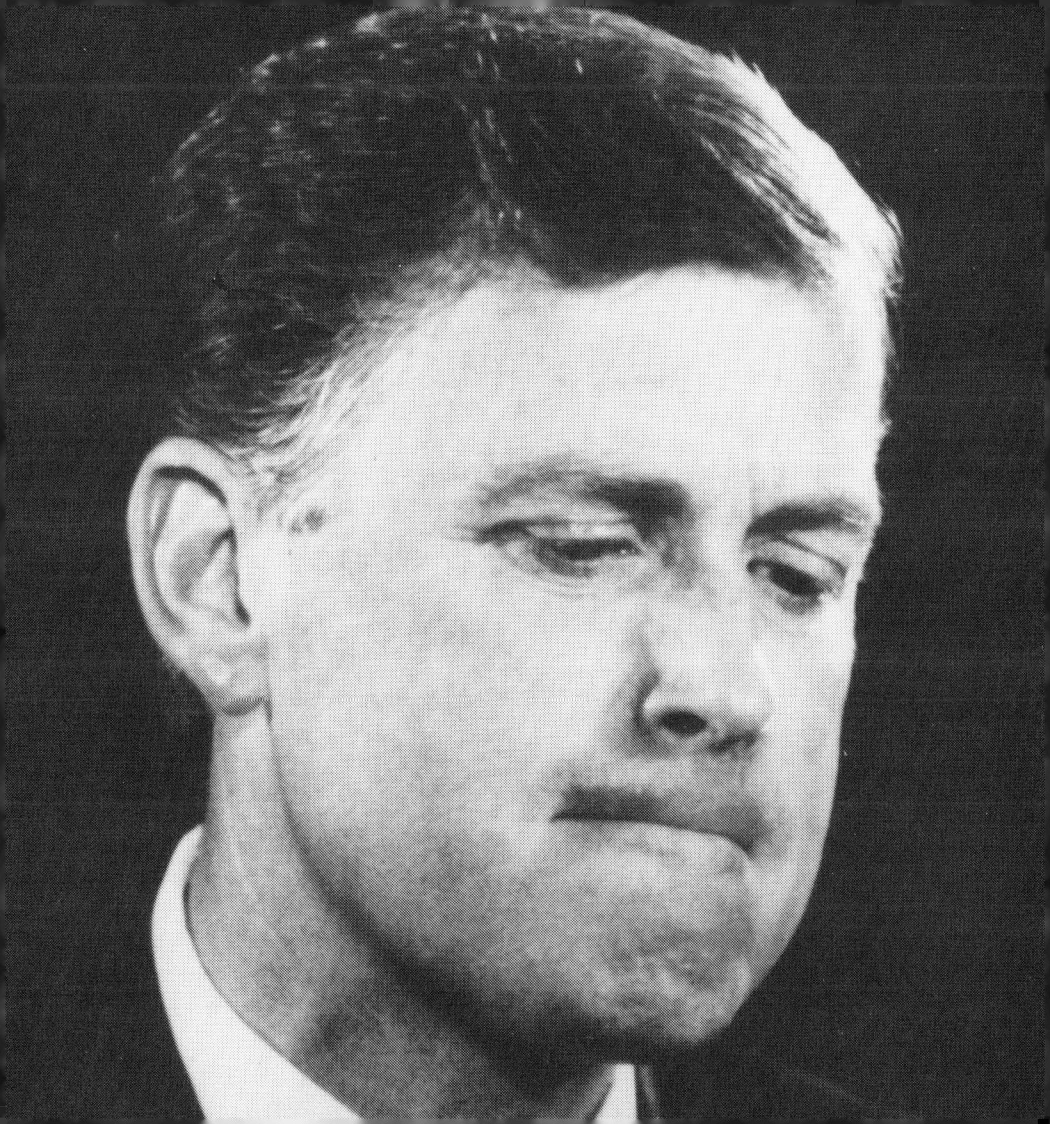

Tt

TAXAS
These are the things that the public thought the Presadent promised the peeple of this state he would not raze when he made his famis plege of "No new TAXAS." I see how it tares the Presadent up when peeple say he lied. He was talking about the state, not the thing! Examin the Presadent's subsecuent record, you'll see there is no new state with this name.

TEMPERMENTAL TYKOON
In Japan, where the word TYKOON comes from, it means a big storm. TYKOONs are dynamic and powerful forces that sweap across the poletical lanscape. Their dynamic, unpredictable nature makes them appear almost TEMPERMENTAL, and also makes them potentially dangerous. Usualley, they blow themselves out before they have created too much damadge.

TRIKKLE DOWN

I thought I was the only one this happened to. Offen, as I left the Sennet Mens' Room, I'd sneak a look down at my pants leg to see if it was really noticabul. Then, one day, Presadent Reagen said something about he dident think it was such a bad thing, and suddenly all the guise in Congres were talking about it. That made me feel better, like I wasn't the only one after all. The only problem was, with everybody talking about it, I had to learn to spel it!

SPELING HINT:

When it happens, it sort of *TIKKLE*s, dosent it? (You dont have to really think so: its just a memmory aide!) Now add an "*R*," and you've got it licked!

TRUST

This is one of the most important words in my poletical vocabularry. Without this, and the income I get from it, I would have to get a job.

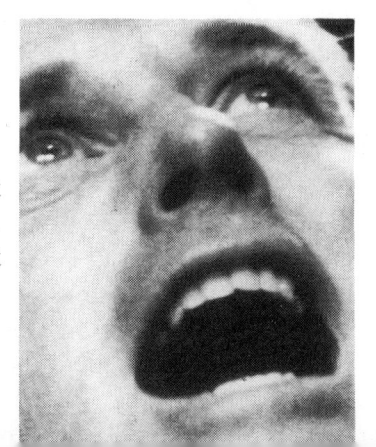

Uu

U is one of those very special leters like A and I—its a single leter that spels a word!

UN
What is an UN? you may ask. The UN is a vital international organization. It is the country club of nations, where diplomats from around the world come to meet and wear suits instead of the funny-looking clothes they wear back home and go to cocktale parties and get parking tickets they never have to pay for. I am not imprest with this organization, but George is an UNman—he worked here once. He still invoaks its name to give speshal emfasis to causes he feels strongly about. Things like housing, edjucation and helth care. I have offen herd him reffer to all these as UNimportent.

UNCUMBENT
A poletician who has lost rellection, but before the end of his turn.

UNEMPLOID
The Presedent told me statistics on the UNEMPLOID are blown out of perportion. I think he's rite. I've been on the CAMPAIN trail, speaking at business roundtables and in corporate auditoriems, and when I ask how many peeple at these companies are UNEMPLOID, no one razes their hands. I'm glad I dident run into any of them. The Presedent says the UNEMPLOID are agenst our rellection bid. They seem pretty organized—you even get payed to join. I know they have ranks, but I don't think they have to wear their uniforms, and you dont have to due any real work, either. No wonder its so popular. It sounds sort of like the National Gard. I'm eeger to lern more about this groop. The Presedent told me if things dont turn around by the fall, we may get a chance to due some first-hand reserch. Sound POLETICS, Mr. Presedent—If you can't beat 'em, join 'em!

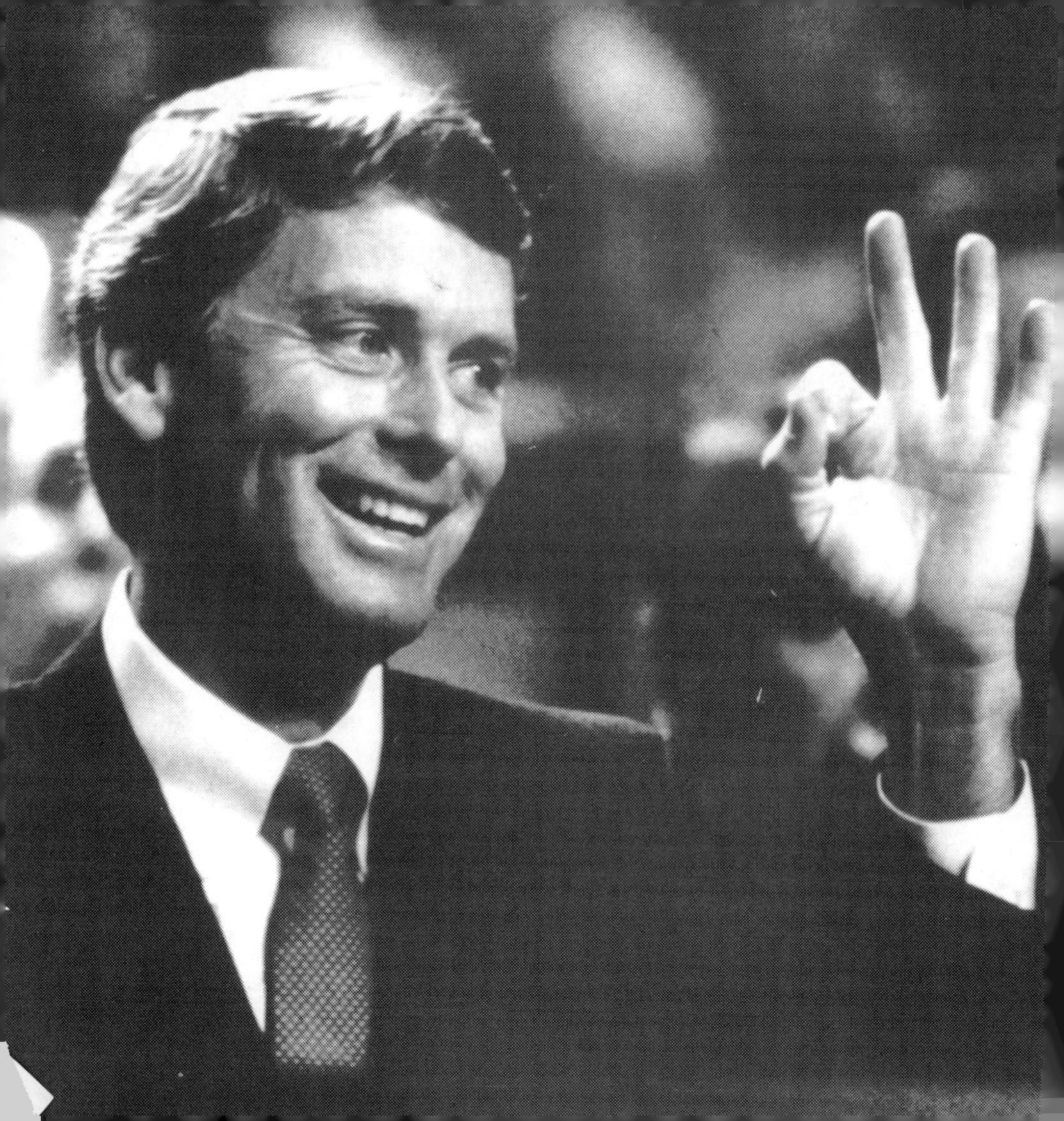

Vv

VALUSE
Don't bother me now, I'm busy making VALUSE a major campain isshue, and I've got the Presedent firmly on bord. Our critics say this isn't a real isshue, but rest assured VALUSE stands for something very important here at the Whitehouse: a *V*ision of *A*ppocalypse and *L*awlessness we *USE* to get votes.

VEAP
January '88. I see from my notes this is when I first herd about the "VEAP." I thought it was some new lightwait army vehicle. I felt kinda dum making that misstake, but my staff said at least I was rite about the lightwait part. But its no army boondoggie—it turns out a VEAP is a *V*ery *E*masculated *A*pprentice *P*osition. You dont know what that means? Join the club—I've got the language boys at State working on a translation!

79

W w

When I was first lerning my ABCs, I really apreciated this leter. By the time I got to W, I'd alreddy had to memmorize more than 20 others. I felt like one more and my head would explod! But when the teacher said Double U—it was like a revalation! I already knew U, so I just had to put the U's together! And after I lerned to use only too instead of three U's in a row, it was a snap! Too this day, I have a soft spot in my hart for this leter.

WARSHINGTON D.C.
This is our nation's center of goverment, comprized of the twin cities of WARSHINGTON A.C. and D.C. In D.C., the *D*istrict of *C*olumbia, crack deelers and South Ammerican cartells run everything. That's the WARSHINGTON you always here about, and that's two bad, because here in WARSHINGTON A.C., *A*mmerica's *C*apitel, there are many beautiful buildings and famus monuments.

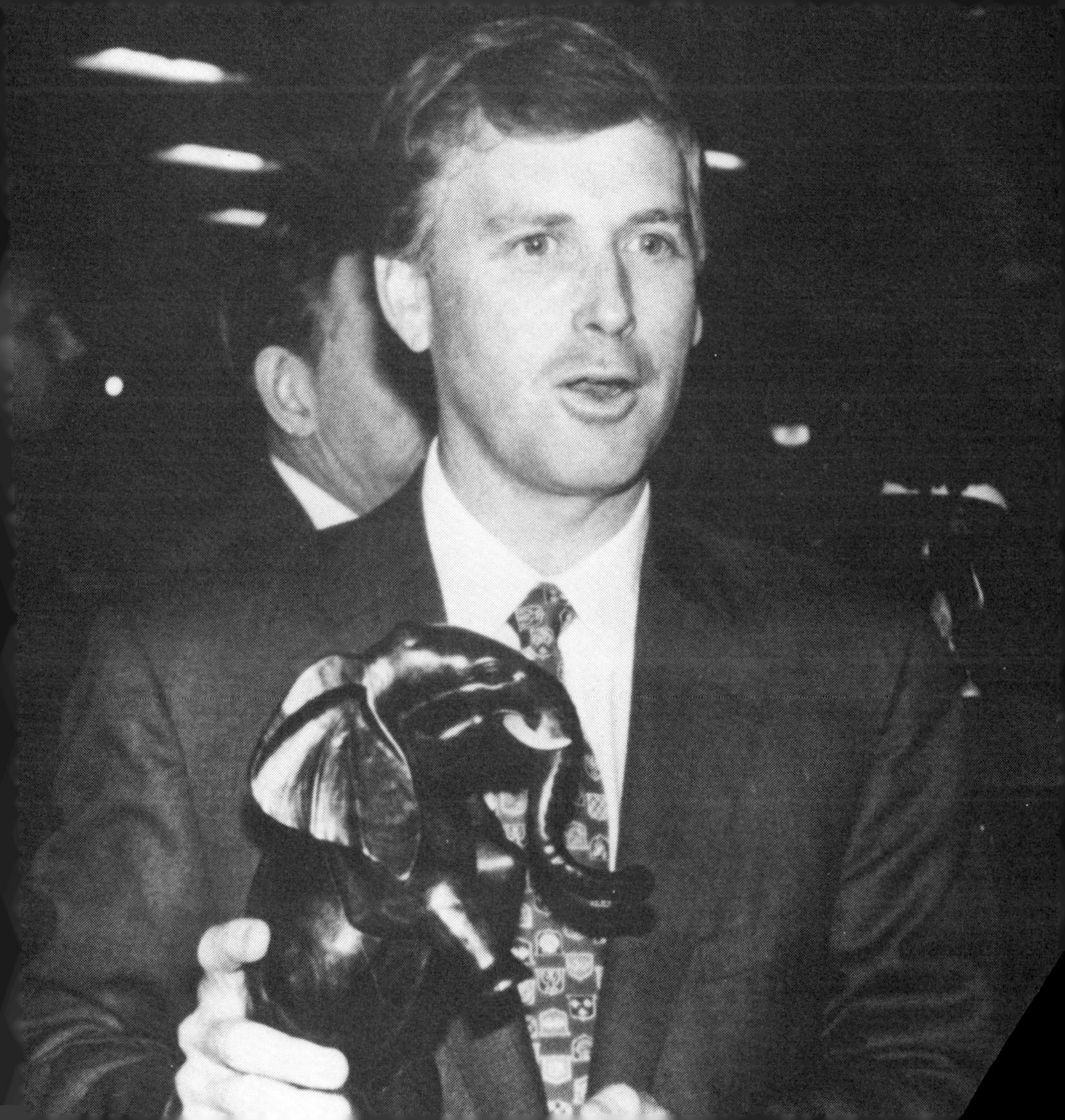

W

WELLFAIR

This is what you call an oximoron, wich means something that contradicks itself. I gess that makes WELLFAIR really moronic, because usualley it takes more than one word to due that. It sometimes takes me as much as a paragraph.

This situation makes WELLFAIR a challange, because even if its speled rite, its wrong. To help you rememmber, think of the program as *WELL* and *FAIR*, and quote Madona: Knot!

WHYVES

WHYVES are very important, poleticaly speaking. How can a voter feel like having a relationship with a man who himself seems incapable of having a relationship? For a married man in ofice with a WHYVE, however, it is relatively eazy to have a relationship with a voter.

MARALIN is my WHYVE, and she is a valuble aset, poleticaly speaking. She is what we call my better have. There's always something she better have, she tells me, and I better get it for her.

Xx

You mite think we don't like this leter at the Whitehouse, what with poronography and X-ratings and stuff. Not so. Take a look at the definitive economic plan we've sent to Congres, the plan that lays out the details of the Presadent's GROATH PAKAGE. *X is the leter we used to show exactly how much money this pakage will cost.*

X-PATRIOT MISSEL
We realize that for Patriot Missels, the months since the conclusion of the PURSIAN GOLFF CAMPAIN have not been eazy. When the parades ended, many saw littel oportunity in sivilian life. Lingering questions about their battlefield conduct left many imbittered. For humanitarium purposes, we have helped a large number of them move overseas, where they are establishing thriving comunities of X-PATRIOT MISSELS in third-world countries around the globe.

GETTING SPELING HELP

Before you can improve your speling, you've got to be ready to admit you need help. I attend a twelve-step program at Spelers Annonymous that helps me deal with my problem one day at a time. Geting up and talking about it with others who understand what I'm going through has done wonders for my self-esteam. And suport from my groop members has been fantastic.

Y y

YELLSIN

I just don't trust this guy. Everything about him shouts "bad" to me. But the Presadent has ordered me to lern to spel his name in the interest of sementing tyes between our too countries. I guess I will have to think of some way to jog my memmory for this one.

85

Zz

Z is the leter they use to show someone is sleeping. It got a real workout during the last addministration. If your Z is tired and wants to sleep, dont let it lie down on its side—peeple will think its an N!

ZENOFOBIA

ZENO is a country in South Afraca I think, or somewhere in the Mideast, like maybe around Canton, Ohio. We are not afraid of this or any other country. Let those who critisize our preferense for staying home and watching TV, rather than venturing abroad to meddle in ZENO's internal affares, not confuze our lazyness and lack of cohearint polecy with fear.

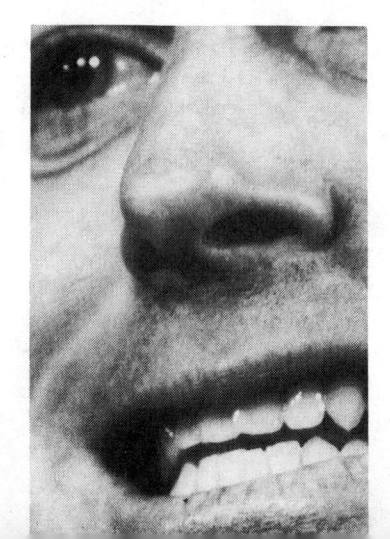

ZERO OPTION
I dont have the details yet, but I think this is one of the Presadents new edjucation initiatives. At exam time, students can choose this, and automatically get a zero without having to take the test. I sure wish we had this when I was in school!

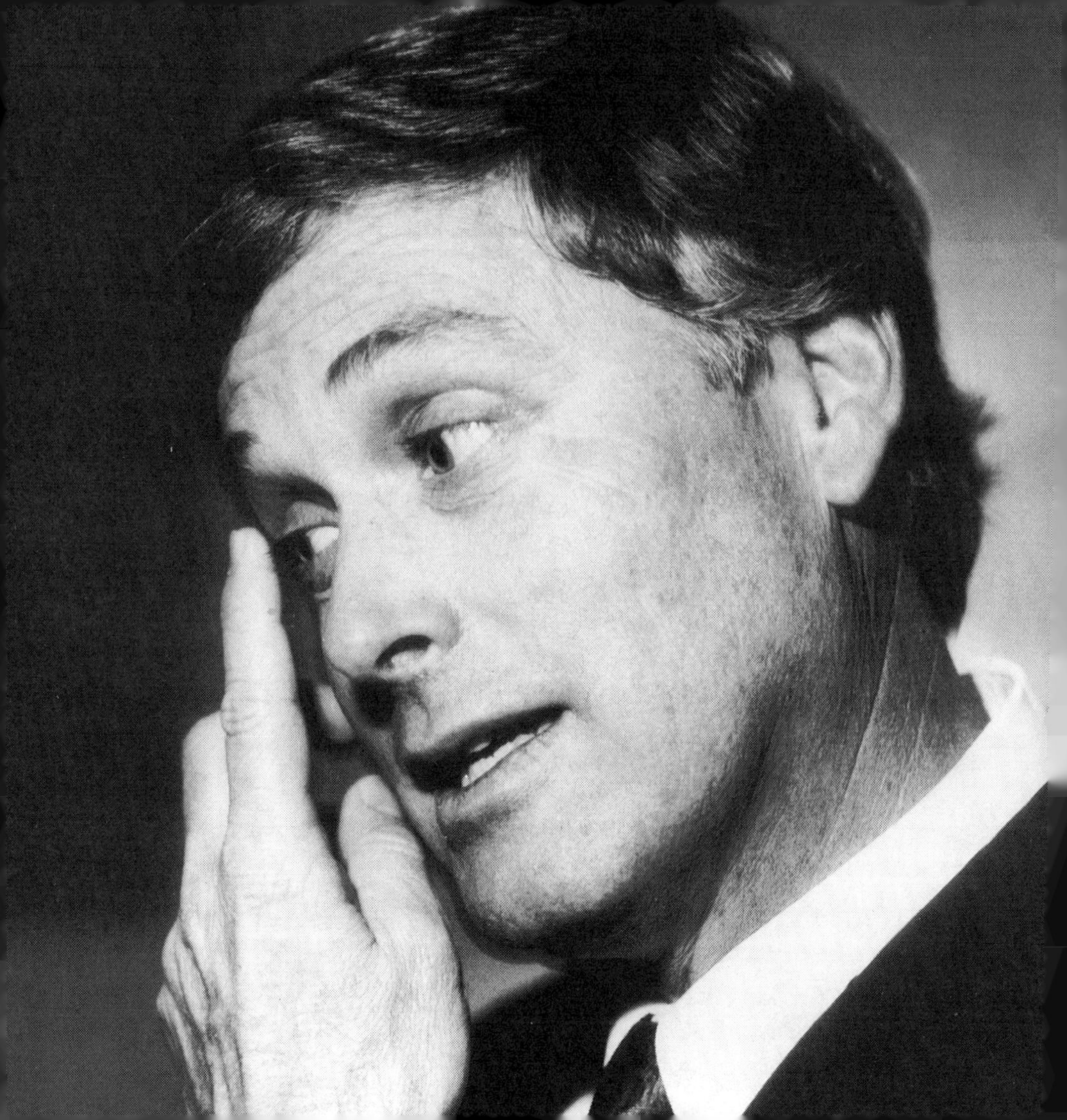

An Ammerican Alfabet

The alfabet is like our wonderful melting pot of Ammerica—Leters working together to build words, each knowing its place in the alfabet, with A always the first and X always the last. And each leter, no matter what part of the alfabet its from, has an oportunity to be in a word—even if you don't see two many Zs or Xs in prominent positions in importent words.

SPEL CHEK

If you don't know which leter to use, rememmber: Even if you choose one at random, you've got a 1 in 26 chance of geting the rite one—that's much better odds than in roulette or the lottery, and peeple have won lots of money playing both of those!

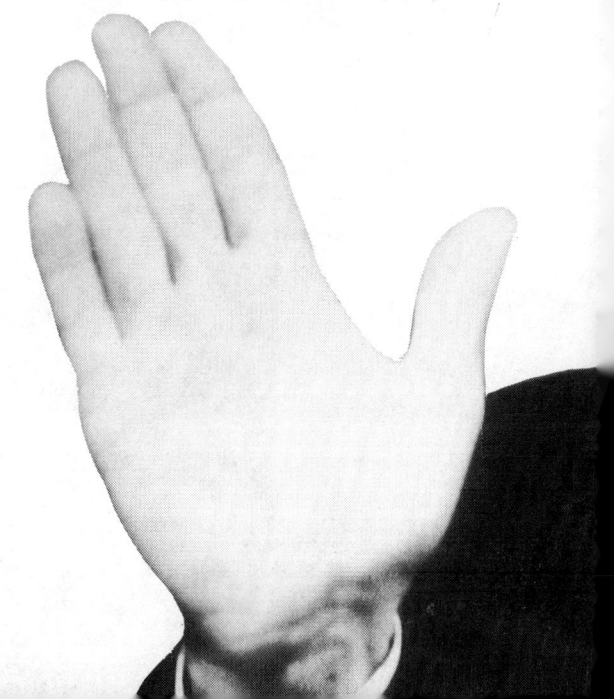

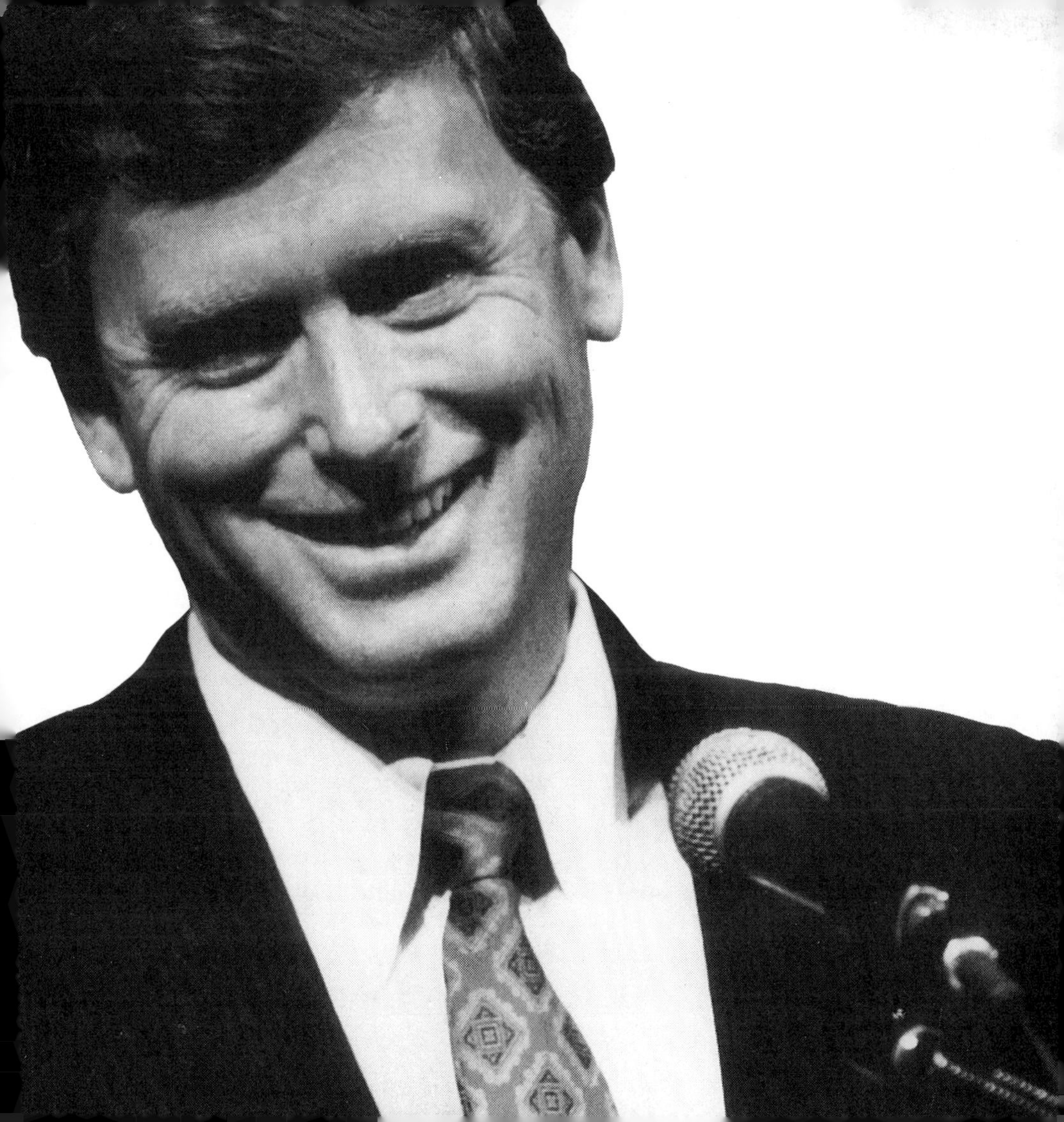

Photos appearing on pp. 4, 10, 15, 31, 81 used courtesy of Reuters/Bettmann Newsphotos.

Photos appearing on pp. 11, 32, 53, 57, 71, 84 used courtesy of UPI/Bettmann Newsphotos.

Photos appearing on pp. 9, 64 © 1992 by P. F. Bentley, Black Star.

Photos appearing on pp. 19, 86 © 1992 by Dennis Brack, Black Star; pp. 21, 29, 38, 42 © 1988 by Dennis Brack, Black Star; pp. 68 © 1989 by Dennis Brack, Black Star; p. 54 © 1990 by Dennis Brack, Black Star.

Photo appearing on p. 45 © Jack Affleck, Sygma.

Photo appearing on pp. 46 © Laura Sikes, Sygma.

Photos appearing on pp. 41, 52, 55, 85, 91 courtesty of AP/Wide World Photos.

Photos appearing on pp. 49, 63, 75, 78 © J.L. Atlan, Sygma.

Photo appearing on p. 60 © A. Tannebaum, Sygma.

Photos appearing on pp. 61, 89 © R. Maiman, Sygma.

Photo appearing on p. 66 courtesy of Miguel Solis, Sygma.

Photo appearing on p. 23, 34 © 1991 by Rick Friedman, Black Star.

Photos appearing on pp. 73, 77 courtesy of Markel-Liaison,
© by Gamma.

Photo appearing on p. 87 courtesy of Gamma-Liaison,
© Cynthia Johnson.

Photo appearing on p. 88 courtesy of Ken Touchton,
Gamma-Liaison.